This book
belongs to':

Rita Mohan
930-4034

In
Defense
of
the GURU
PRINCIPLE

In
Defense
of the GURU
PRINCIPLE

Andrew Cohen

MOKSHA
PRESS

1999

Copyright ©1999 by Impersonal Enlightenment Fellowship
P.O. Box 2360, Lenox, Massachusetts 01240 USA
Printed in the United States of America
Design by Moksha Press
Printed on recycled paper

Moksha Press Cataloging
Cohen, Andrew, 1955 Oct. 23-
In defense of the guru principle / by Andrew Cohen.
p. cm.
ISBN 1-883929-27-X
1. Gurus. 2. Gurus—United States—Biography.
3. Cohen, Andrew, 1955 Oct. 23- 4. Spiritual life. I. Title.
BL1241.48   291.61—dc21

Contents

The Guru principle is a force of Love and evolution that cannot and will not rest until we *all* have finally and irrevocably dropped our infatuation with the deadly illusion of a false and independent sense of self.

Andrew Cohen

Foreword

by Yvan Amar

From the very first moment I met Andrew Cohen in Jerusalem in 1987, a constant recognition has been alive in me: here is a man who can lead people to the threshold of their being. Over the years, Andrew has accepted different invitations to come to France and speak to large audiences of people, including gatherings of my own students, and my recognition of him has always been unwavering. Andrew is a rare being, an authentic spiritual teacher, who is as impeccable with his actions in life as he is with his words and ideas on the teaching stage.

I invited him to France because of this and because of what it would mean to earnest seekers in our country. But it was also because I started to love the man, the friend. Straightforward, simple, clear and direct, he is a man who is capable of an uncorrupted relationship to life and to friends, a man who can be relied upon, a man whose presence and word have *weight*.

Indeed this is the first and paradoxical meaning of the word *guru*, built on an Indo-European root meaning heavy, weighty, that which has gravity or gravitation. In fact, this word is more concrete, more material than its spiritual and abstract destiny would lead one to believe. A *guru* is a man of *weight*, because having incarnated reality in his body, he is *heavy* with that reality, and as such exerts a force of gravitation, of *attraction*—the *Self-appeal* of all great teachers—on those who approach him.

A teacher such as Andrew is a man capable of an enlightened relationship, a relationship centered on a *universal* endeavor, an endeavor that stems not from personal desire. Whenever someone approaches him, they are taken into that enlightening process, regardless of their own personal agendas. Not everybody is prepared to enter such a relationship, not everybody is prepared to directly experience the *Guru principle*.

The response of the individual or social ego to the eternal challenge of Dharma that such a man represents is dramatic. There are not two ways to teach. God does not speak to man, God speaks to God in man. The drama of a teacher is that while he is speaking to God in man, he still has to face and meet with the man himself—and not always for the best.

Throughout the years, what I have witnessed in Andrew is

compassion: that infinite capacity to explore again and again, as if for the first time, the ultimate priority in life. He listens to the suffering man without compromise, responding with compassion from WHAT IS, here, now, always, everywhere.

Such a man can awaken in many the taste for an adventurous life, a life where courage is synonymous with faith, a life where love is synonymous with consciousness.

Preface

by Professor James R. Lewis

"You missed the mark," I thought, as I finished reading Andrew Cohen's essay "In Defense of the Guru Principle." Despite my disagreement with the central thesis of his argument, I had been stimulated by the essay and sat lost in thought, gazing out the window as the plane began its descent into Hartford. Having studied religious controversies for the past fifteen years, I felt confident that an insistence on spiritual purity was *not*—as implied in Cohen's discussion—the kind of issue that would evoke antagonism from the larger society. At the same time, however, I was having difficulty putting my finger on exactly what it was that made Cohen such a controversial figure.

A specialist in nontraditional religions, I had flown to the East Coast to attend an academic conference. I was also making this trip to meet with a few religious groups headquartered in the northeastern United States. One of the primary organizations I was interested in visiting was Andrew Cohen's Impersonal Enlightenment Fellowship. I had been aware of the fellowship for about a year. Over the course of that period of time, I had been familiarizing myself with the group's teachings and with some of the attacks that had been made against Cohen. My initial evaluation was that this conflict flowed out of some of the same factors that had affected a broad variety of different groups. In the case of the Impersonal Enlightenment Fellowship, Cohen and his movement were suffering at the hands of an irresponsible mass media more interested in exploiting sensationalism than in the less-than-titillating truth. This general evaluation was reinforced by the material I had read during the long plane ride from California.

During my visit with the Impersonal Enlightenment Fellowship, I was frankly impressed. Not only was it clear that Andrew Cohen led a simple, unpretentious lifestyle congruent with his teachings, but I also found Cohen's students uniformly mature, likeable and mentally alert. I had studied many spiritual movements at close range, but in all those years had never encountered a group with which I felt more comfortable.

Over the course of my stay, I had a number of conversations with students about their ongoing problems with "bad press," specifically the difficulties they were encountering getting their responses to various critical articles heard. In one instance, for example, they discovered that a *spiritual* magazine had published a one-sidedly negative article about Andrew Cohen (without bothering to call him to check the reliability of the story). The fellowship subsequently contacted the magazine and requested an opportunity to prepare a formal response. After receiving a "maybe" answer, they rushed out a short piece (the original "In Defense of the Guru Principle"), only to have it ultimately rejected as being "too critical"—as if Cohen's measured response was inappropriate after his being completely trashed in the very same pages. Other periodicals in which negative pieces had appeared were refusing to print even letters to the editor from Cohen's students. It was as if some shadowy, *X-Files*-like conspirator in a smoke-filled room had called all of the relevant publishers with instructions to "bring down" Cohen.

As I reflected further, it began to dawn on me that what was going on here was something other than what I had first supposed. While a number of critical pieces had appeared in the mainstream press, it was becoming increasingly evident that the real nexus of the controversy was to be found within the spiritual subculture itself. Although his critical analysis of this subculture has been couched in relatively mild terms, Cohen has breathed life into his critique by establishing a community of students who have responded to the call to awaken. Had he merely been a critical voice, or had members of the Impersonal Enlightenment Fellowship quietly pursued enlightenment without stepping on anyone else's toes, the response might have been different. In combination, however, the dual thrust of Cohen's challenge fundamentally calls into question the vested interests of the "spiritual establishment" —that informal network of organizations, publications and teachers who have become comfortable with something less than the goal of ultimate freedom.

I began to see that the attention of the mainstream media had obscured the basic source of the controversy. Long after the *Los Angeles Times* and the *Boston Globe* will have forgotten about Andrew Cohen, the spiritual establishment will continue to attack him. This "establishment" might be nothing more than an informal network of people who know people who know yet other people. In whatever way it is organized, however, it is clear that it has closed ranks against Cohen and is actively trying to discredit him. And, contrary to the conclusion I had reached in my initial evaluation, the attack has been provoked by the very reason indicated by Cohen.

In the present compilation of essays, Andrew Cohen articulates some of the central themes of his teaching in the context of an analysis of the role of the spiritual teacher.

As a way of amplifying the original article, "In Defense of the Guru Principle," two other pieces have been incorporated: "Thoughts on the Student/Teacher Relationship" and excerpts from an earlier work, *Enlightenment Is a Secret*. In all of these pieces, Cohen makes clear that the *Guru principle*, in the proper sense, is nothing less than the call to awaken itself. This call, when presented powerfully and without compromise, will always be unwelcome to a world asleep in the dream of ego.

INTRODUCTION

Ever since the very beginning of my teaching career, people have responded to my message in extreme ways. That is because I have never been able to divorce the experience of love from its absolute demand.

True love and the absolute freedom that it brings demands everything from us. As long as we want to have anything for ourselves, even freedom itself, we will not find true emancipation in this life. True love demands everything, and Liberation, which is its reward, can only be ours when we are willing to sacrifice even that.

What has always intrigued me is that so many people appear to be interested in the experience of love while they so often seem mysteriously able to avoid its implications. This is part of the reason why, I think, in recent years so many have been able to spend a significant amount of time in the company of powerful spiritual teachers, attracted to and absorbed in the experience of love, without that experience necessarily having a deeper impact upon them than one of feeling better.

Many have been drawn to me initially because of the experience of love that they have felt in my presence. And while the majority may be more than satisfied with that, for me it has never been enough. I have never been able to allow those who have come to me to settle merely for the experience of feeling better. While bliss indeed may temporarily create the illusion that all is well, in most cases, underneath that bliss still lies the demon of ignorance, ready to strike as soon as the bliss fades or when the ego is challenged once again.

If the experience of love and bliss is not merely a superficial event, then in that experience must be the revelation of the emptiness of a separate or personal self. That means, therefore, that ideally bliss becomes not the possession or mere object of fascination for the ego, but that ocean of being within which the ego loses its balance and all points of reference.

It is because the demand to drown and truly lose oneself in that ocean for eternity is not made often enough that so many seekers end up satisfied with being mere voyeurs of their own Self, rather than living expressions of it. Because the attachment to the ego and the world of becoming is so strong, most seekers feel deeply threatened by the possibility of drowning forever.

The course of my life as a teacher has been defined by my continuous insistence that the experience of love and bliss is meaningless when it is not supported by a life lived with true integrity. Integrity, in a life based upon the pursuit of freedom, is the unconditional willingness to renounce all that has been discovered to be false, wrong and untrue. Ironically, it is because of this that I have been the object of much controversy.

In retrospect, I can see that even from early on this was my message, implicitly if not directly. Little did I know that this would often pose what appeared to be an almost overwhelming challenge for many. The integrity, or lack of it, in the manner in which one lived one's life became an issue of fundamental importance for those who gathered around me from the very beginning. In fact, for those who became one with me in spirit, it soon was expected that integrity or purehearted motivation be the expression of one's response to the experience of love and bliss. It is precisely this that has simultaneously attracted some and repelled others.

PART 1

In Defense of the Guru Principle

A Controversial Figure

"Everybody out there is waiting for you to make a mistake," the late Suzanne Segal told me one rainy afternoon in Marin County, California, in 1994. Suzanne had recently become a spiritual teacher in her own right and was on the verge of becoming famous as a result of the publication of her book *Collision with the Infinite,* which was a vivid description of the evolution of her own spiritual journey. Over the last few months we had become friends. She had sought me out, as she had many other teachers, for guidance in helping her to understand her own powerful experience of, as she repeatedly referred to it, "no self." "Yes," she said, "they're all out there just waiting for you to make a wrong move." She was amazed at what a controversial figure I'd become simply because I was daring to set a standard at a time when all of the most renowned Gurus and Masters had fallen on their faces as a result of countless scandals and revelations of impropriety. Not only had I dared to call a spade a spade when my own Guru had been repeatedly dishonest and duplicitous, but to make matters worse, I had naively assumed that the spiritual

world at large would welcome with open arms my unwilling-
ness to compromise the truth *for anyone*. How wrong I was.

My insistence that any man or woman who dared to
assume the role of Master or Guru had an inherent obliga-
tion to the universe to walk the straight and narrow was met
with self-righteous indignation. My simple protestations that
if Enlightenment was to mean anything then any Master or
Guru worth their salt had to be able, ready and more than
willing to *live* their own teachings impeccably—because it
was their *duty* as Master or Guru to do this—only brought
down upon me even more controversy. "Who the hell does
he think he is?" was the popular refrain. What made matters
even more bizarre was that it seemed, as Suzanne was telling
me that rainy afternoon, that many people desperately *wanted*
me to fail. The very fact that I was successfully holding a
high standard for myself and those around me seemed to be
creating an unacceptable tension in the spiritual world that
only incited anger and the hope that I would fall on my face
as so many other spiritual teachers had. For example, the
editor of a popular spiritual magazine expressed interest in
writing about the work that I was doing if and when there
was a scandal. Several years later, after I had moved with my
students to a beautiful property in the Berkshire mountains

of western Massachusetts, my heart shuddered one morning when I was informed that my own mother, who I already knew was writing a book about me, had eagerly asked a mutual friend, *"Has Andrew slept with any of his students yet?"*

Not for Everyone

What was the impetus behind this ferocious response to my teaching work? It sounds ridiculous, but it's true: *nonduality.* My message has always been extremely simple: to be free, to be *Enlightened,* means that the inner and the outer have become ONE. "One" means *no difference* between the message and the messenger, no difference between talk of nonduality and the expression of the personality. It means One and One and forever *only One.* This teaching, that the inner and the outer must become One if spiritual evolution is to mean any-thing at all, simultaneously inspires *and* frightens, uplifts *and* shocks even the most sincere seeker. Why? Because in the time we're living in, talk of Oneness is acceptable and even sought after, but the demand for the personality to *conform and surrender to that Oneness alone* is seen as ludicrous. In fact, it is seen as repressive and even fascistic. By who? By the ego, of course. Who else would protest the absolute common sense behind such a plea for simplicity, sanity and real integrity of being? But what could Enlightenment be, if not the final merging of the inner revelation of Oneness and the outer expression of the human personal-ity? "NO!" the ego screams in defiance. "What about ME?! I exist too! I *deserve* to exist! . . ." But you see, the Self Absolute hears nothing of these protests, for it recognizes *only* ITSELF. *All else is always recognized to be perfectly unreal.* And the role of the Master, in fact the actual function of the Guru principle, is the very manifestation *in time and space* of that force of Love Absolute that recognizes only Itself. The true meaning of compassion is, in the end, the unwavering ability to awaken in others the very consciousness of that Love Absolute that recognizes only Itself, that unites the inner and the outer in nondual simplicity.

Is the path to Enlightenment for everyone? Of course not. Who except only the most serious among us would venture so far beyond the known? Who would dare to venture *that* far beyond the status quo of the materialistic, self-aggrandizing world of difference that is samsara? No, the path of Enlightenment is not for the faint-hearted, nor for any except those who have come to the point in their own evolution where they have no doubt that they want to be free from the chains of ego *in this very life,* and who are willing to pay the price. What is the price? Ego death.

Ego Death Is Not a Game

Ego death is not a game. The part of the human animal that is vicious pride, that is the tenacious desire to *have* and to be separate and unique in the face of God, is what "ego" is. Ego is the irrepressible, ever defiant, always-knowing-better hubris that *never* wants to submit unless there is something to be gained for itself. That ego is the one and only enemy of Enlightenment, of True Love in this world of multiplicity and mystery in which we all find ourselves. And the Guru principle is that very force of Love that's only function is to destroy the vicious pride within us that is always the enemy of Love. The Guru principle is that force of evolution itself that tirelessly, helplessly and uncontrollably never wavers.

Not all spiritual teachers are teachers of Enlightenment. In fact, not all Masters or Gurus are teachers of Enlightenment—which means teachers of *ego death*. This is not a small point. In fact, this is quite significant to consider, as these days almost *everybody* seems to be speaking about Enlightenment. Teachers of all kinds, each in their own way, are speaking as if they are experts on this most delicate of all matters. Hence the incredible confusion about Enlightenment and ego death. You see, what is so often these days taught in the name of Enlightenment and ego death is in reality neither Enlightenment nor ego death.

The deadly serious nature of the genuine quest for liberation from ignorance and fear must be acknowledged honestly and humbly when face-to-face with a Master in whom the Guru principle has been awakened. Indeed, entering into a conscious and intentional relationship with a Master in whom the Guru principle has been awakened is a serious matter. That relationship is certainly *not* a safe and secure environment for the ego. Only if we sincerely want to be free more than anything else will we have access to the spiritual heart within us that alone will have the power to recognize the Guru principle as nothing more than the call of one's *own* True Self. If that is not the case, the Guru principle will be seen for what it is *but* from the perspective of the ego, which means—it will be seen *as our worst enemy.*

My Own Outrageous Life

My now-estranged mother, who had been my student on and off for three years early in my teaching career, proudly told me over dinner that she was putting the finishing touches on the manuscript of her new book—a book which portrays me as a dangerously deluded and frighteningly pathological figure whose insatiable thirst for absolute power over pathetic and weak-minded individuals is couched within the pretense of a passionate interest in the spiritual Enlightenment of humanity. "I've changed some of the facts for dramatic purposes," she said casually. Little did I know that even the conversation we were having at that very moment would itself become, in her book, so distorted as to have no resemblance whatsoever to what was actually occurring between us.

In the ever perplexing story of my own outrageous life, I find myself in a rather unique predicament. Because most Gurus and Masters have indeed used their position of power at times for their own personal gratification, there is an almost unified collective conviction in our time that pure motivation is an *impossibility* in a Guru. That is why even the very word "Guru" (which means "destroyer of darkness") has fallen into such disrepute. Though there has never been a hint of any scandal whatsoever in all my thirteen years of teaching (and even my worst critics struggle with that fact), there has certainly been, from the very beginning, a trail of wounded egos claiming abuse of power. If we play with fire, we will get burned. That is why the path to Enlightenment is not something to be casually played with. Ironically, in my case, the wounding of pride has been called scandalous. But— and this is the whole point—that's my job. It is a sign of the times that there is such a profound lack of understanding of what it actually means to enter into a relationship with a Master in whom the Guru principle has been awakened.

Only *One* Self

"Now tell me about *your* shadow," the powerful therapist-*cum*-Guru asked me one evening over a cup of coffee. He had just humbly and honestly told me in excruciating detail the painful story of the collapse of his role as a Guru and leader of a spiritual community after having ingested an extremely potent hallucinogenic drug. "I don't know what to say," I confessed. It dawned on me that it simply wasn't acceptable not to have, nor to be more than happy to speak in depth about, one's "shadow" if one was a spiritual teacher these days. In fact, in the wake of the rampant corruption of spiritual authority figures in the time we're living in, if one doesn't refer either implicitly or explicitly to having a "shadow," it seems to make one instantly untrustworthy.

Indeed, it is not uncommon to hear spiritual teachers speaking freely and unapologetically about division that exists within themselves. For example, there is a world-renowned Buddhist meditation teacher from California who pleases his followers by proudly recounting the story that his young children are his best teachers because they let him know when he's not being "mindful." "There are different parts of myself," he describes to his audiences. "The part of me that gets angry, I call 'Genghis'; and the part of me that falls asleep when I meditate, I call 'Mr. Sleepy.'" The fact that this kind of fundamental division actually puts people at ease is the very expression of how crazy the whole business of spiritual evolution and Enlightenment has become in the time that we're living in.

But what is Enlightenment all about? *Enlightenment is the realization of One Self, and the death of division and multiplicity within the human personality.* Undivided intention, undivided motivation, undivided action *is the whole point. One* Self—not two, not three, not four—is the goal of all spiritual practice. From the many to the One.

But we live in a cynical time—a time when it seems few even believe that it's actually possible for any human being to express that depth of singularity. In fact, nowadays the implication always seems to be that if one is expressing that depth of singularity, there must be something wrong.

The Guru Principle

The renowned transpersonal theorist Ken Wilber wrote in a letter to one of my students, "Of course, in flatland America, the Master/Teacher/Guru principle is not, and never will be, understood or allowed, so it is a brave group that attempts to introduce depth in the midst of this wasteland."

Even though, as Wilber and others suggest, the Guru principle for many reasons will never be accepted in this time and place, the fact remains that once awakened, it is a force of Love and evolution that cannot and will not rest until we *all* have finally and irrevocably dropped our attachment to, and infatuation with, the deadly illusion of a false and independent sense of self. The Guru principle has never been and will never be "accepted" by the powers that be. The fact is that its passion, once awakened, in any time and place, will always be *too much.*

PART 2

Thoughts on the
Student/Teacher Relationship

Meeting the True Teacher

The Promise of No-Limitation

In the presence of that rare human being who has attained extraordinary spiritual Enlightenment, a tangible sense of expansion of Self can be felt. When someone is living with that much intensity, freedom and love, one recognizes a liberated personality. By their example and in their reflection, one can discover, maybe for the very first time, what it would be like to be free.

In such a meeting, unanticipated experiences involving rare insight and/or exhilarating feelings may occur. An event such as this can shake the very foundation of one's belief system. The effect of this meeting can be so powerful that the individual may suddenly find him- or herself entering into what seems like the most profound relationship that one human being could ever have with another.

What makes the idea of entering into a relationship with a spiritual teacher so enticing and profound? *It is the promise of no-limitation.* But very few people make full use of the unique potential inherent in that promise.

A real teacher always remains true to the fact of no-limitation. A real teacher never wavers from the demand that those who claim interest in Liberation above all else be willing to meet them *fully and completely* in the living experience of no-limitation. *In this challenge, the student comes face-to-face with the true measure of their own desire for Liberation.* That challenge creates a tension which is the gap between the teacher's living example and the student's actual condition. And that tension disappears only when the student fearlessly and courageously endeavors to meet the teacher absolutely, completely and without reservation.

In the true teacher's reflection, any and all attachments to that which is false, wrong and untrue will be revealed. That is why the teacher's living example only becomes superfluous when and if the student equals or surpasses the teacher's attainment. Up to that point, the teacher's living, breathing example is of the utmost importance, for it is in the teacher's reflection that the teaching comes alive and can be clearly seen and recognized. Without the teacher's living, breathing manifestation of the teaching, the ultimate goal of spiritual practice remains lost in vague, superstitious and even dangerously confused notions.

In most cases, even a perfect teaching in and of itself cannot create enough evolutionary tension to thrust the individual into the kind of radical transformation that is necessary for permanent change to occur. That tension is created in the relationship with a true teacher because the student is afforded the unique opportunity of an unusually clear reflection—of actually being able to see themselves without distortion. The relationship with a teacher who is the living expression of no-limitation will make apparent those limiting ideas, beliefs and tendencies that the student compulsively and usually unconsciously imposes upon themselves and on reality as a whole. It is through that association that the student will be able to see very clearly and accurately how and where they are inhibiting their own potential of realizing and ultimately manifesting no-limitation.

No Refuge for the Ego

Rather than striving to fulfill the liberating promise of no-limitation, which is the recognition of *no security* for the ego, most students actually endeavor to *find* security for the ego in the relationship with the spiritual teacher. They allow a relationship of dependence to develop because they are not really seeking for genuine Liberation, but instead are using the relationship with the spiritual teacher to take refuge from the very challenging ordeal of mundane existence.

There is no doubt that taking refuge in the knowledge and power of an extraordinary human being has great benefits. But as great as those benefits may be, their effect will ultimately always express limitation until the student comes to that point in their own evolution when they are finally ready to take complete responsibility for their own life. It is only in assuming that degree of responsibility that the student will be able to meet the teacher in perfect independence.

Indeed, the relationship with the true teacher should offer the ego no security whatsoever and should instead result *only* in the discovery of perfect aloneness, perfect independence and the ultimate fulfillment of one's individuality.

Perfect Independence Allows True Partnership

At the beginning stages of association and relationship with a spiritual teacher, it is reasonable for the individual to seek for affirmation of self, and in that affirmation, healing at a deep emotional level. That experience—the validation of self—*is* the unanticipated and mysterious event that occurs in a real meeting with a true teacher. But that event, instead of becoming an end unto itself, should serve as the foundation for the student's pursuit and ultimate attainment of final Liberation.

Ideally, the healing that occurs in the meeting with the true teacher serves as a catalyst for the simultaneous ending of the past and beginning of a truly unimaginable future. That future is the one-pointed pursuit of the dissolution of all false and deluded notions about the nature of self, and in that dissolution, the birth of a truly liberated human being.

Once again, for this dissolution to occur, absolute responsibility must be taken by the student for their own Enlightenment and everything that this inevitably entails. That means that the individual who wants to be free must come to that point in their own development where they would be willing to give *everything* for the highest attainment. What is that attainment? It is the living, breathing manifestation of perfect Liberation *as oneself*. It is only at that point that the powerful evolutionary potential inherent in the relationship with the spiritual teacher can begin to manifest itself. That potential is the thrilling experience of a dynamic partnership based on a passionate pursuit of and *mutual* interest in the Real.

Trusting the True Teacher

A Process of Osmosis

When someone chooses to become involved with a spiritual teacher, a process of osmosis begins to occur within that individual at a very deep psychological and emotional level. This osmosis takes place both consciously *and unconsciously*, and its effect is much greater than most people tend to be aware of.

When an individual becomes seriously involved with a spiritual teacher, every aspect of the teacher's personality—gross and subtle—is absorbed at the deepest levels of the student's psyche. Indeed, it is a largely unknown fact that it is not the depth and breadth of the teacher's teaching, but the actual condition of the teacher *as a human being* that in the end has the most significant influence on the student.

The Door to Liberation

The individual who seriously seeks for a Teacher, Master or Guru wants to find a mentor who they feel is truly worthy of being Teacher, Master or Guru. There is always the desire in the seeker to ultimately find a spiritual mentor who they perceive as being perfect, or if not literally perfect, then as close to perfect as is humanly possible. Why is this necessary? Because it is imperative for the seeker to have confidence not only in the spiritual attainment of the mentor, but more importantly, in the *integrity of the mentor as a human being*. Without this confidence, it is unlikely that a seeker will allow themselves the profound and rare liberty of utterly letting go at the deepest levels of their being.

The experience of trust in the teacher allows a radical shift in consciousness to occur. The effect of that shift in consciousness is that the student now feels that they have a center, a very strong center, the experience of which enables the student the luxury of being able to trust, maybe for the very first time, in life itself.

Ideally, the trust found in the relationship with the spiritual teacher serves as the bridge from isolation and separation to direct conscious recognition of perfect interrelatedness. It is in this way that the relationship with the spiritual teacher can serve as a door to Liberation.

PART 3

Three Excerpts from
Enlightenment Is a Secret

The Teacher Is an Outward Manifestation of Your Own Heart

Some people feel a yearning and a burning that is a kind of quiet agony. This is when it becomes painfully obvious that something absolutely fundamental to our very existence is unresolved, incomplete and unsatisfied. Some begin to seek, pray, read and meditate to try to satisfy this yearning and bring this pain to an end.

When you find a real Teacher, there is a movement that is most precious, very delicate and inconceivably sacred. The Teacher is an outward manifestation of your own heart, and responds only to that pull that is already there within you. Like two lovers, the attraction can become unbearable.

When the yearning within you and the open heart of a real Teacher come together, it is a very delicate moment.

A Spontaneous Event

If you are lucky enough to find your Teacher, in that meeting you will actually begin to see before your very own eyes yourself becoming aligned to your True Self. You will actually feel it happening. This is a spontaneous event in which you begin to feel closer to who you always have been. You will feel more like who you *are*. You will feel a freedom from identifying yourself with other people and outside events. You will realize a natural condition of being. In this experience there is a profound resonance in a great harmony. There is ecstasy in this release. When you truly meet your Teacher, this is what happens.

When You Are at One
with an Enlightened Teacher

If you are at one with an Enlightened Teacher, then time and space cannot come between you. One with the Teacher means one with yourself. Your True Self cannot be inhibited by time and space.

When you have experienced and understood the teaching of Enlightenment—*you have to live it.* When you begin to live the teachings without conditions, then you become the Teacher. What the Teacher teaches and what you do will be one and the same. When you are ready and willing to accept the teaching of Enlightenment without conditions and are ready to give every breath of your life to living that Enlightenment perfectly, then and only then will you and a true Teacher of Enlightenment be one.

Biography

Andrew Cohen is not just a spiritual teacher — he is an inspiring phenomenon. Since his awakening in 1986 he has only lived, breathed and spoken of one thing: the potential of total liberation from the bondage of ignorance, superstition and selfishness. Powerless to limit his unceasing investigation, he has looked at the "jewel of enlightenment" from every angle, and given birth to a teaching that is vast and subtle, yet incomparably direct and revolutionary in its impact.

Through his public teachings, his books and his meetings with spiritual leaders of almost every tradition, he has tirelessly sought to convey his discovery that spiritual liberation's true significance is its potential to completely transform not only the individual, but the entire way that human beings, as a race, live together. In sharp contrast to the cynicism which is so pervasive today, yet with full awareness of the difficult challenges that we face, he has dared to teach and to show that it is indeed possible to bring heaven to earth. This powerful message of unity, openness and love has inspired many who have heard it to join together to prove its reality with their own lives, igniting an ever expanding international revolution of tremendous vitality and significance.

OTHER BOOKS BY ANDREW COHEN

Freedom Has No History
Enlightenment Is a Secret
An Unconditional Relationship to Life
Autobiography of an Awakening
My Master Is My Self
Who Am I? & How Shall I Live?
The Promise of Perfection
An Absolute Relationship to Life
The Challenge of Enlightenment

IMPERSONAL ENLIGHTENMENT FELLOWSHIP
CENTERS FOR THE TEACHINGS OF ANDREW COHEN

Founded in 1988, Impersonal Enlightenment Fellowship is a nonprofit organization that supports and facilitates the teaching work of Andrew Cohen. It is dedicated to the enlightenment of the individual and the expression of enlightenment in the world.

For more information about Andrew Cohen and his teaching, please contact one of the following centers or visit the IEF website at www.moksha.org.

UNITED STATES

INTERNATIONAL CENTER
P.O. Box 2360
Lenox, MA 01240
tel: 413-637-6000 or 800-376-3210
fax: 413-637-6015
email: moksha@moksha.org

BOSTON CENTER
2269 Massachusetts Avenue
Cambridge, MA 02140
tel: 617-492-2848
fax: 617-876-3525
email: 73214.602@compuserve.com

NEW YORK CENTER
311 Broadway, Suite 2A
New York, NY 10007
tel: 212-233-1930
fax: 212-233-1986
email: info@faceny.org

EUROPE

LONDON CENTER
Centre Studios
Englands Lane
London, NW3 4YD UK
tel: 44-171-419-8100
fax: 44-171-419-8101
email: 100074.3662@compuserve.com

AMSTERDAM CENTER
Oudeschans 46A
1011 LC Amsterdam, Holland
tel: 31-20-422-1616
fax: 31-20-422-2417
email: 100412.160@compuserve.com

COLOGNE CENTER
Elsasstrasse 69
50677 Cologne, Germany
tel: 49-221-310-1040
fax: 49-221-331-9439
email: 100757.3605@compuserve.com

STOCKHOLM CENTER
Roslagsgatan 48nb
113 54 Stockholm, Sweden
tel: 46-8-458-9970
fax: 46-8-458-9971
email: ac.center@swipnet.se

OTHER CENTERS

SYDNEY CENTER
479 Darling Street
Balmain, Sydney
NSW 2041 Australia
tel: 61-2-9555-2932
fax: 61-2-9555-2931
email: 105312.2467@compuserve.com

RISHIKESH CENTER
P.O. Box 20
Sivananda Nagar, Distr. Tehri Garhwal
U.P. 249192 India
tel: 91-135-435-303
fax: 91-135-435-302
email: iefrish@nde.vsnl.net.in